INTRODUCTION

I teach predominantly willow furniture, but this book is not about willow. It is about tapping into your own imagination and creating rustic furniture from what is available. Your only limitation is your imagination and imagination is in your head.

In this book I want to get across to you the art of somethingness (the opposite of nothingness) that transcends rustic furniture and offer the idea that we can do anything with anything and can create something out what often is considered nothing or trash.

We live in a world that is based on throwing things away. It is a time when things are built with the idea that they will last for a year or less and then are bound for the landfill. In this age of obsolescence, when something breaks down it is cheaper to buy a new one than to fix the old one...if one year of existence can be considered old.

In this book we will do three projects:
• The Sassy Chair, a chair of sassafras and willow
• A simple bench of sassafras
• A bakers rack or potting table out of sassafras

I am often asked where I find sticks. My pat answer is that they grow on trees. These projects can be made from a variety of different woods. In each case we will be using material that is growing in the wild and readily renewable or waste wood, like that often found on the side of the road or bound for the dump.

—Bim Willow

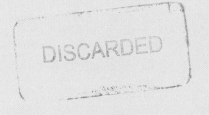

THE SASSY CHAIR

Tools needed (l-r): rasp, 16 oz. hammer, 8 or 10 oz. hammer, bypass cutters for nails, pruning shears, tape measure, and loppers. Spiral ardox galvanized nails needed: 4p, 6p, 8p, 10p and 16p; 1" brads.

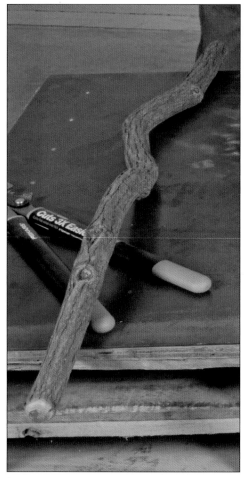

For this project, I'm using sassafras. Cut two sticks 1-1/2" – 2-1/2" diameter, 4-5 ft. long, and preferably crooked to add interest. These are to be used for the back legs.

Cut two sticks, 1-1/2" to 2-1/2" diameter, 25" long, also with character, as the front legs.

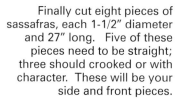

Finally cut eight pieces of sassafras, each 1-1/2" diameter and 27" long. Five of these pieces need to be straight; three should crooked or with character. These will be your side and front pieces.

The ends should all be dressed. With pruning shears, trim off the cut edges from each end of the sticks.

Rasp the newly trimmed edges to create a smoother look. Remember to trim the edges of each of the frame pieces this way throughout your project.

Lightly rasp the rough bark to bring out the color of the sassafras and make it smoother.

Hold a back leg and front leg upright to see which way you want the crooks and angles to face each other.

If the front leg is crooked or curved, the top end should bend toward the outside of the chair.

Lay one back leg and one front leg parallel to each other, with the bottom ends even (aligning them to the edge of the worktable is an easy way to do this). Make sure the crooks in the back leg bow towards the back. Place one of the 27"side pieces across these legs, so that the top edge of the stick is 4"up from the bottom of the leg, and extended 2"off each side. (When working with green wood, it is essential not to nail too close to the end or to trim too close to where you have nailed so that the wood will not split. Two inches is considered safe, so I refer to this as the "2-inch principle.") Nail the side piece on to the back leg using a 10p nail.

Turn the front leg so that the crook is sticking up in the air. When the chair is finished, this will allow for more seat room and space to attach the arm. Nail the side piece on to the front leg, 4"up from the bottom edge with a 10p nail. The side piece should extend 2" past the leg, like you did with the back leg.

Nail the straight side piece to the front leg with a 10p nail, so that the top edge of this stick is 14" up from the bottom of the leg, with a 2" overhang on each side.

The other end of this side piece should be nailed to the back leg so that its top edge is 13" up from the bottom of the leg, again making sure that 2" overhangs beyond the leg.

Add a 1"diameter diagonal brace to the side, high at the front leg and low at the back leg, between the horizontal braces.

Cut off excess, leaving 2" minimum overhang.

You have now finished one side of the chair.

This process is repeated for the other side, with the legs on opposite sides from each other. Nail the bottom brace on to the back legs, 4" up from the bottom, leaving 2" overhang on each side.

Nail the brace to the front leg in the same way.

Still on the front leg, place the upper side piece 14" from the bottom of the leg and nail in place.

Before nailing the upper side piece to the back leg, place the first side you completed on top of the side you are working on. Line up the side brace and the back leg that you are working on with the completed side.

Carefully remove the finished side and nail the side piece into the back leg.

Add a 1" diameter diagonal brace, keeping it high at the front leg and low at the back leg, between the horizontal braces. Nail in place with 10p nails.

Cut off the excess.

Now that both sides are assembled, we're going to add the front brace. For this piece, use a 1-1/2" diameter stick that is 27" long and as straight as possible. This will be used to establish your seat.

You can hold the front brace between your legs while you nail into the side piece. Make sure that your side braces are on the outside.

Place this front brace above the top side brace, and nail into the leg with a 10p.

Nail the other side.

Choose one of the 27" pieces that is crooked or has character to become your lower front brace. Place it between the front legs and above the bottom side braces. Attach one side to the front leg with a 10p nail. Check to make sure the front legs are parallel to each other.

Finish nailing the front piece.

Stand the chair up. Move back legs inward to about 19" apart.

Add a 23" brace at that bottom of the legs, above the side diagonals.

Nail the brace to the back leg using 10p nails.

Add a second back brace. Place it above the top side brace. Nail one side into a leg using a 10p nail.

Check to make sure the back legs are parallel.

Nail the other side into the second leg.

Now we're going to add a seat brace. This piece needs to be straight and 1-1/2" to 1-3/4" thick. Allowing for at least a 2" overhang on each side, mark the length...

...and cut off excess using a chop saw.

Place this seat brace a palm's width from the back leg.

This should be placed 18" back from the front brace.

...and then the other side, using 10p nails.

Nail into the top side brace on one side...

Between the side pieces, we're going to add another seat brace that is lower and will help create a comfortable seat. Place this brace halfway between the front brace and the seat brace that was just added. Measure and mark this piece so it will fit in between the side pieces.

Cut to size with a
chop saw.

Place in between
the side pieces...

...and nail through the outside of the side piece into the seat brace using a 16p nail on each side.

Choose a narrow stick with a slight curve. Place it on top of the side pieces behind the front legs so that the curve dips down and there is a 2" overhang on one side. Using 10p nails, attach to one leg...

...and then the other.

Cut off the excess if necessary, leaving a 2" overhang.

Rasp the edges of any cut wood that may have been missed.

Add a diagonal brace to help stabilize. Choose a 1" diameter brace long enough to extend from just in front of the top brace on the back leg, diagonally to the top of the bottom brace behind the front leg on the opposite side. Secure each end with a 10p nail into the leg.

Nail the diagonal braces together where they cross using an 8p nail.

Add another diagonal brace going in the opposite direction. Nail into the front and back legs with 10p nails.

This is the result so far.

Allowing for 2" overhangs, cut off the excess length from both diagonals.

Now we're going to add the rungs to this ladder back chair. Using pruners and a rasp, finish one end of a 1-1/4" to 1-3/4" diameter stick.

Place one end of the stick against the inside of the back leg and mark where the stick would butt up to the inside of the other back leg. This first rung should be approximately 12" up from the top of the side rails.

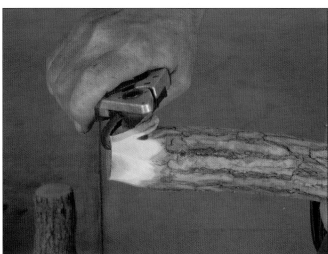

Cut, finish the end, and hold it in place between the two back legs.

Because we're working with imperfect material, angles need to be cut in order to create that perfect fit.

Trim the angle with loppers.

A much better fit.

Holding this rung in place, nail through the back leg into the rung using a 16p nail. Repeat on the other end of the rung.

Add second rung using the same steps as before. Position it 12" above the first rung.

Because of the free form nature of this chair, the rungs do not have to be parallel.

Repeat process with third rung, using a curved or crooked stick with character.

Now it's time to add the arms. Choose two gnarly, curved pieces, approximately 2" in diameter. Place them on top of the front legs so they extend to the back legs. Check to make sure the curves don't interfere with seating.

Cut the arms so that they extend 5-6" beyond the front leg and 3" behind the back leg. Finish the cut edges.

Hold the first arm in place and nail into the top of the front leg using a 16p nail.

Nail the other arm into the front leg.

Making sure that the arm is parallel to the seat, nail the arm into the back leg with a 16p nail.

Eyeball this second arm to make sure it is level with the first.

Nail into place.

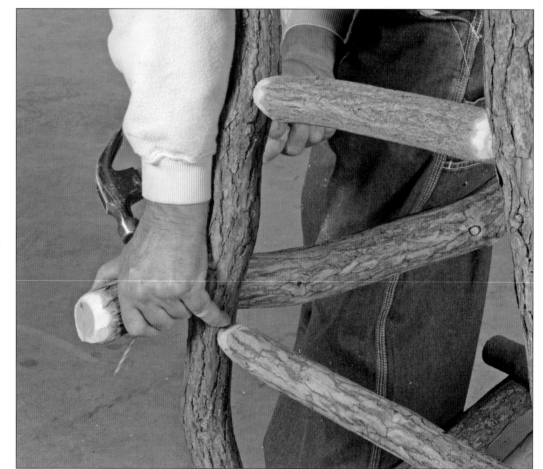

Using a 6p nail, add a 3/4" straight piece of willow on top of the front brace.

Cut off excess wood to match the front rail.

The project so far.

Now we're going to add the last diagonal brace in the front. This is placed behind the front legs. Behind one front leg it should start at the bottom, resting on the previous cross brace. Nail it into the back of the front leg with a 10p nail. . .

...with second nail into the diagonal brace below.

At the other leg the front brace comes between the side seat rail and the side diagonal brace.
Nail through the side rail into the brace.

Cut off the excess, remembering the 2" principle.
Now we're ready to add the willow seat.

Bend a 5' long piece of 1/2" diameter willow into an "L" shape. Place the curve of the "L" into the center of the seat so that the curve hits the back seat brace. Using 4p nails, secure the willow to the center seat brace. . .

...and then to the back seat brace.

Nail to the back seat brace at 1" apart.

From here, we will be creating a "flair" design in the back. Following the same steps as before, secure a second piece of willow to the center seat brace, 1-1/2" apart from the first willow.

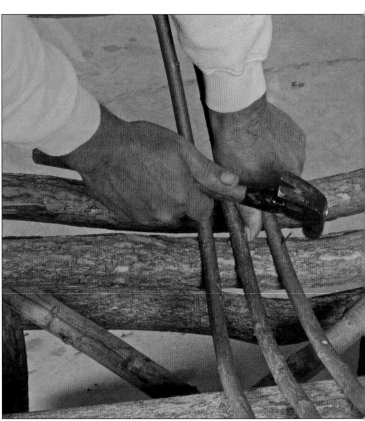

Secure a third piece of willow to the center seat brace, on the other side of the center willow at 1-1/2" apart. Nail to the back seat brace at 1" apart.

Repeat these steps until the seat is filled. This will take approximately 10 pieces of willow.

Using 4p nails, attach the willow to the second rung and then the top rung. This can be done while spreading the willow into a symmetrical fan pattern...

...or, as in this case, going off to one side in an asymmetrical way.

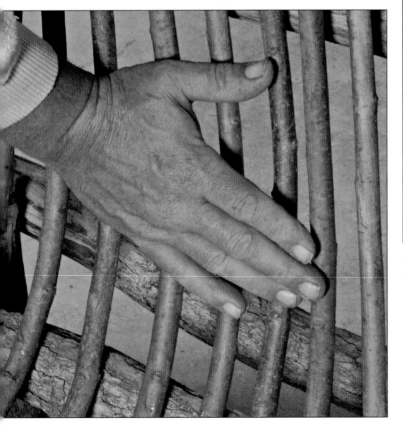

While attaching the seats, keep in mind that you want to keep the sticks flush with each other for comfort.

Because I chose to go off to one side, I've run out of rungs to nail into to, so I nailed to the legs.

Those benders I nailed into the leg, now come around
and are nailed into the back of the back legs.

Trim off the excess willow from the top of the back.

Nail them also to the top rail.

Leave at least 2" away from any nail so that the willow won't split later, but the maximum length is an artistic option.

The project so far.

The project so far.

Clip off the excess seat willows, just behind the willow stick attached to the top of the front brace.

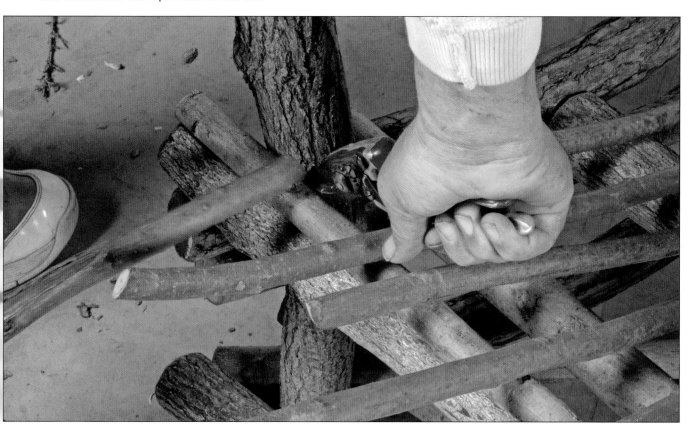

The seats should fall right into place. If they don't, you can push them down...

...and nail each in place with a 4p nail through the front willow piece.

Now nail all the seat willows to the seat brace that was curved, behind the front legs.

The following five pictures show The Sassy Chair complete.

GARDEN BENCH

Pick out a piece of wood for the bench seat. I usually buy or find wood that is 12" wide, a minimum of 1-1/2" thick, and 40" in length. Choose four 1 ½"- 2 1/2" diameter sticks; cut two 16" long and two 36".

Rasp any rough spots from the face of the bench seat and the edges.

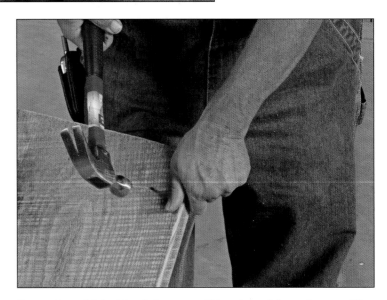

Determine which side of the seat will be viewed from the top. The method I am demonstrating to attach the front legs is called 'blind nailing' in which nail heads will be hidden. On the bottom side of the seat, nail a 10p nail about 2" in from the corner that will be the front edge of the bench. Nail only about 1/2" into the seat.

Nail a second nail into the opposite front edge corner in the same manner.

With a pair of bypass cutters for nails, cut off each of the nail heads at an angle.

Lay the bench seat on the ground with the cut nails sticking up in the air. The four legs are 1-1/2" to 2-1/2" diameter sticks. Two are cut to 16" and two are cut two 36". Center one of the 16"sticks onto a nail head and pound the stick onto the nail.

Pound the stick until is flush with the bottom of the seat.

Repeat with the other 16"piece onto the other nail.

Tilt the bench seat so that the back of the bench seat and the bottoms of the front legs are touching the ground. Place a 1-1/2"diameter stick across the bottom of the front legs, to become a front brace.

The stick is a palm width's up from the bottom of the first leg, and will have a 2" overhang beyond the legs.

Nail the front brace to the first leg with an 10p nail.

Using the same steps, check to make sure the legs are parallel to each other, and nail the front brace in place.

Cut off the excess; maintain the 2"principle for overhangs.

Flip the bench so it is laying upside down with the legs up. Working at the back of the legs, place a front diagonal brace from the joint of the first leg and seat, up to where the horizontal front brace connects to the second front leg. Nail the diagonal onto the second front leg using a 10p nail.

Finish nailing the diagonal brace.

Cut off the excess.

Attach the remaining 36" stick as the fourth leg.

Stand the bench up and straddle it, holding the bench seat as level as possible with your legs. Hold one of the 36" sticks onto the back of the bench seat, in line with the front leg. If the 36"stick is curved, turn the curve to it flares out toward the back of the bench so it won't interfere with seating. Using a 10p nail, reach down and nail this leg into the back edge of the seat. The bench should stand on its own now.

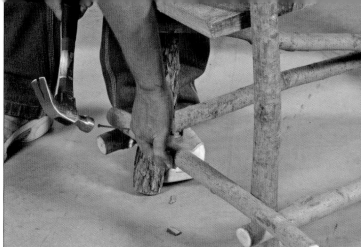

Using a 1-1/2" diameter stick, nail a back horizontal brace to one back leg. Use a 10p nail and place the brace about a palm's width up from the ground. Place your foot behind the bottom of the leg to keep it from moving while you hammer.

Place a 1-1/2" diameter stick from front to back, on top of the horizontal braces. Attach this side brace to the front leg using a 10p nail.

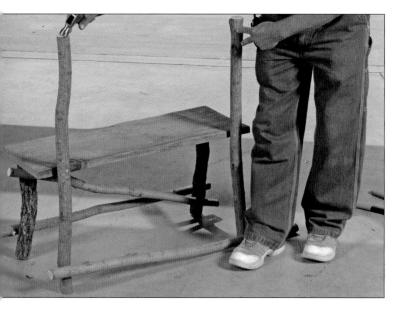

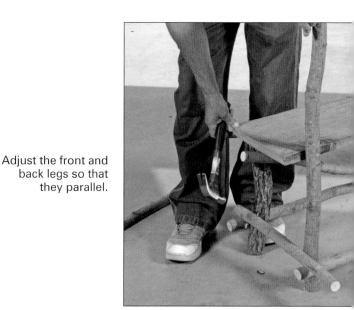

Adjust the front and back legs so that they parallel.

Straighten the back legs so they are parallel to each other...

...finish nailing the back horizontal brace.

Finish nailing the side brace to the back leg.

54

Repeat these steps on the other side of the bench.

Repeat these steps for a diagonal brace on the opposite side of the bench.

The project so far.

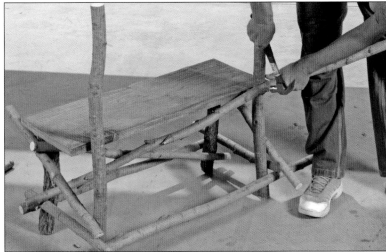

To stabilize the bench, place a long, 1" diameter diagonal through the back of the bench, so that it rests behind the front leg on top of the side horizontal brace. Using a 10p nail, attach it to the inside of the back leg.

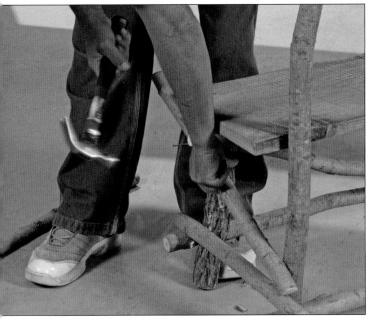

Place a 1-1/2" diameter stick at an angle, from above the side brace on the back leg, to the top of the front leg. This will become the side diagonal brace. Keep in mind the 2" principal. Using a 10p nail, secure to the front leg, and then to the back leg.

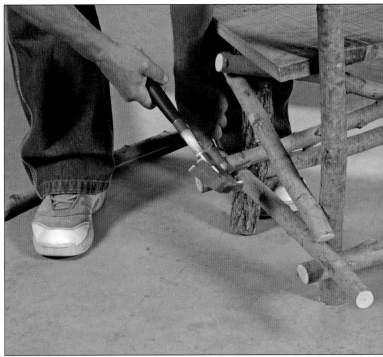

Finish attaching this diagonal by nailing to the inside of the front leg.

Repeat these steps to create another diagonal that connects the remaining front leg and back leg.

...then the other side.

Using loppers, cut off excess from all of the 1-1/2" sticks. Always leave at least a 2" overhang from the nail so that the wood will not split in the future.

Cutting off any excess is an artistic option.

Place a 1-1/2" to 2-1/2" stick on top of the back legs. In this case, I have chosen a straight piece, but a crooked, gnarly piece will work beautifully, as long as it is placed so that the crooks and bends don't interfere with sitting comfort. Nail one side into place with a 16p nail...

Rasp the cut edges for a more finished look.

To finish the bench seat, frame the edges with willow. Using 3/4" to 1" thick willow, cut to the exact length of the bench side.

Using another willow stick, trim the front edge, overlapping the cut edge of the willow trim on the side.

Holding the cut edge of the willow even with the front edge of the bench, nail into place, using 6p nails. Again, remember the 2" principle.

Place nails 6" – 8" apart across to secure the front trim willow.

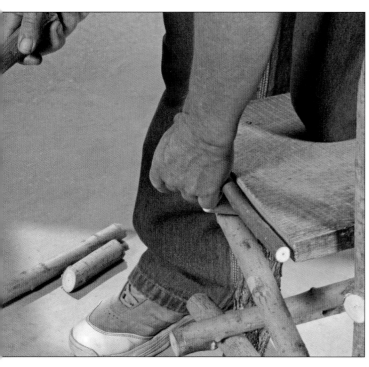

Repeat these steps to trim the other side of the seat.

Cut the excess so it's even with the edge of the willow side trim.

The frame is now finished. Decorating the frame with willow is where artistic expression takes form. When bending willow, do not force it into too sharp a bend quickly or it will snap. When adding willow, maintain the 2" principle on all cut ends. Use willow that is at least 1/4" thick; smaller pieces will split when nailing and break more easily after the piece is built. I usually choose 3/4" to 1" thick willow. Position the thick end behind the side brace.

...and also to the side diagonal under the bench.

Secure the thinner parts of the willow wherever it meets the bench frame with a 4p or 6p nail.

Bend the willow in front of the bench back, placing the thin end behind the opposite back leg.

Using a 4p or 6p nail (depending on the thickness of the willow), secure the willow to the bench back...

I am choosing to start the second piece of willow behind the front brace and curve it around the back of the bench...

...threading it through to the front of the bench back.

Continue adding willow and nailing into place.

Secure this piece of willow, bending it as you work into its final position.

In some cases, in order to secure the willow trim and stabilize the structure, you may need to nail two pieces of the willow together.

The project so far.

Make sure that the willow is securely fastened to the bench.

For this project, I have chose to start all of the willow on one side and develop an asymmetrical design. Try each piece of willow in a number of spots before nailing. Let the bend and placement of each stick evolve into your personal 'look'.

Trim off the excess willow, leaving at least 2" beyond each nail. I cut the ends at angles as part of the artistic look.

You may or may not wish to trim the top ends from the willow on the back of the bench. In this case, I have chosen to butt the angular pieces of willow into one of the curved pieces that loop over the back of the bench. With pruning shears, trim one of the angular pieces so it butts into the looped willow.

Using a 4p or brad, nail through the looped willow into the abutted end. Repeat these steps for the remaining angular pieces.

If there are back pieces that cross each other, nail them together with a brad nail.

The finished bench.

THE BAKER'S RACK OR POTTING BENCH

To build a potting bench, a/k/a baker's rack, you will need 2 slabs of wood, one 24" wide and one 10" wide, each at least 1" to 1-1/2" thick. Cut both to 40" long. Using four 1-1/2" to 2-1/2"diameter sticks, cut two 40"long pieces as back legs and two 32" pieces as front legs.

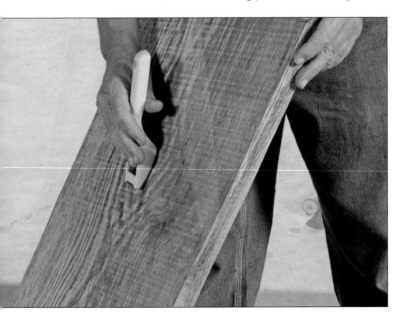

Rasp the top and bottom of the slabs, as well as the cut edges, to make them smooth and take out any marks or stains.

Choose which side of the 24"slab you would like to be the tabletop of the potting bench. Flip this piece so the top of the tabletop is facing down. On the bottom of this piece, nail a 10p nail about 2" in from the corner that will become the front edge of the bench. Nail only about ½" into the top. Nail a second nail into the opposite front edge corner in the same manner. With a pair of bypass cutters for nails, cut off each of the nail heads.

Lay the top on the ground with the cut nails sticking up in the air. Center one of the 32"sticks onto a nail head and pound the stick onto the nail. Pound the stick until it is flush with the tabletop.

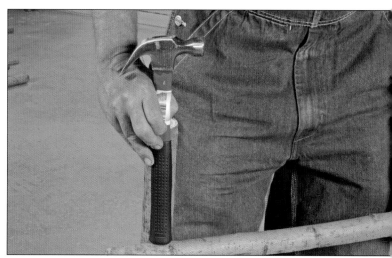

Nail into place about 5"-8" up from the bottom of one leg.

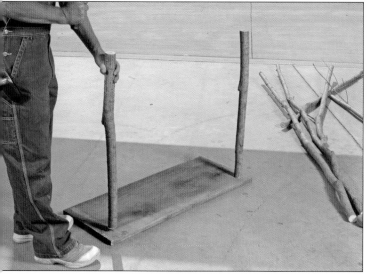

Repeat on the other corner.

Lift the brace up so it is horizontal, and use your hammer handle as a ruler to measure the space from the bottom of the foot to the horizontal.

Place a 1-1/2" diameter stick, across the bottom of the front legs, to become a front horizontal brace. This piece needs to be as straight as possible to accommodate a shelf.

Lift the unattached end of this horizontal brace and position it using the measurement from the hammer handle on the first leg.

Check to make sure the legs are parallel to each other. Secure using a 10p nail.

Brace the angle end with your foot and nail this angle brace into the leg using a 10p nail.

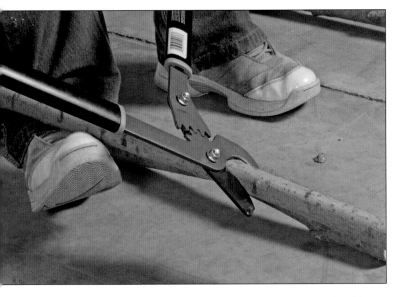

Using loppers, cut two 1-1/4" to 1-1/2" thick sticks at 45% angles to be used as angle braces.

Finish by nailing the angle end into the tabletop with a 6p nail.

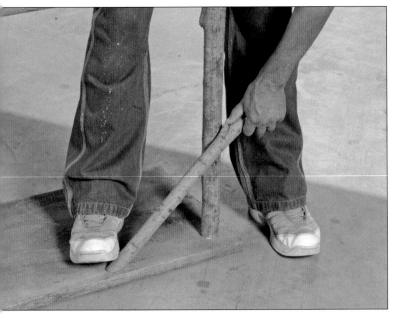

Place the 45% angle flat against the underside of the tabletop and angled out so that it crosses the leg.

Add an angle brace to the opposite side in the same way.

Cut off excess from the horizontal brace on both ends, leaving a minimum of 2"overhang from the nail.

Nail the second back leg in place, again making sure the tabletop is level.

Cut off excess from the angle braces, using the 2" Principal.

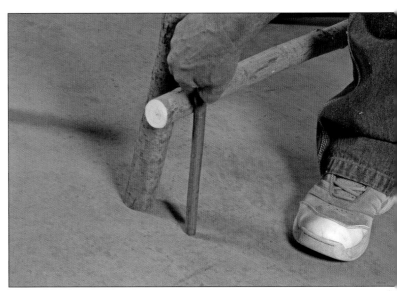

Measuring from the ground up to the top of the front horizontal brace. Mark it on a piece of scrap willow.

Hold the table up so that the tabletop is as level as possible. Place a 40" back leg against the back edge, in line with the front leg, and nail into place using a 10p nail.

Cut the scrap piece to length. This will become your pattern used to make sure the bottom braces are all the same height, so that the bottom shelf will be level. Because of the different thicknesses of sticks, be sure to measure to the top of the brace, not the bottom, when making this pattern.

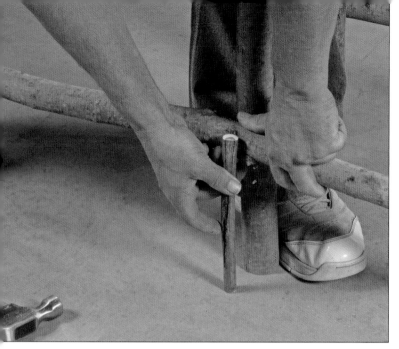

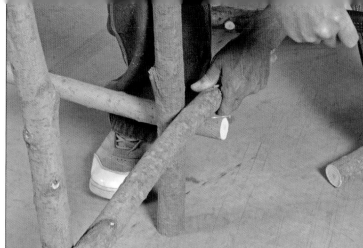

To add a horizontal back brace, place a 1" diameter stick on the back of the back leg so that the top edge of it is level with your pattern stick.

Adjust the front and back legs so that they are parallel to each other, then nail the side brace to the remaining leg.

Using a 10p nails, nail the back brace to the back legs.

Cut off the excess from the side braces...

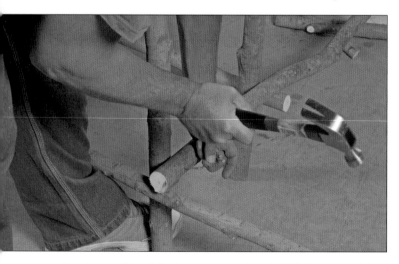

On the outside of the legs, lay another 1-1/2" diameter stick across the top of the two horizontal braces on the side as a side brace. Nail one end to the leg with a 10p nail.

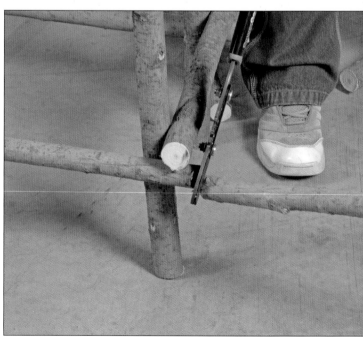

...and the horizontal braces. Repeat these steps on the other end of the table.

Using a 1-1.2" diameter stick, create a diagonal side brace from the front table edge to the top of the side brace. Nail the top end in place first...

Cut off the excess from these diagonal braces.

...then the lower end, again, keeping the 2" principal in mind and using 10p nails.

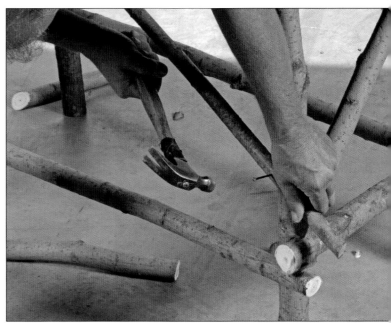

Attach a 1-1/2" diameter stick to the back leg just above the tabletop using a 10p nail.

Repeat on the other side.

Nail the other end into the opposite back leg above the horizontal brace.

Cut off the excess from the back diagonal.

The project so far.

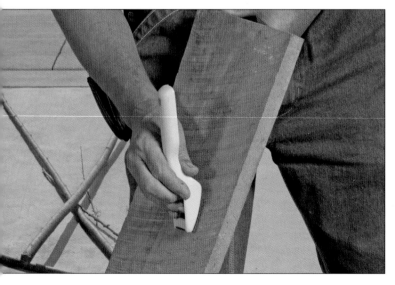

Rasp the smaller shelf if not done earlier.

Lay it on top of the back legs so that it is parallel to the front edge of the large tabletop, centered from side to side, and doesn't extend back further than the outermost braces in back.

Using 10p nails, nail one side through the top into the leg.

Check to make sure the shelf is positioned right and nail the shelf into the other leg.

To trim the edges of the tabletop, use 3/4" to 1" diameter willow. On one side of the tabletop, line the willow up with the back edge, and nail every 6"-8" towards the front edge using 6p nails.

Place another piece of trim willow across the front edge of the tabletop, extending it beyond the side edge.

Using pruning shears, cut the excess of the willow off even with the front edge of the tabletop, pushing down on the excess end of the willow to make the cut cleaner. Repeat this process on the other end of the tabletop.

Use 6p nails every 6" – 8" across the front edge.

Cut off the excess willow flush with the side edge on both sides.

Trim out the top shelf in the same manner.

The project so far.

Building the bottom shelf will take about 18 pieces of willow, each 3/4" – 1" diameter. These will be trimmed to match after half are nailed in place and the trimmed ends will be used to finish the shelf if they are long enough. Place the first piece abutting the front and back legs, resting on the front and back horizontal braces. Position so that there is a small overhang in front. Use 4p or 6p nails to secure to the horizontal braces.

Add additional pieces of willow about 1" apart and parallel to the first. Nail in place with 4p or 6p nails.

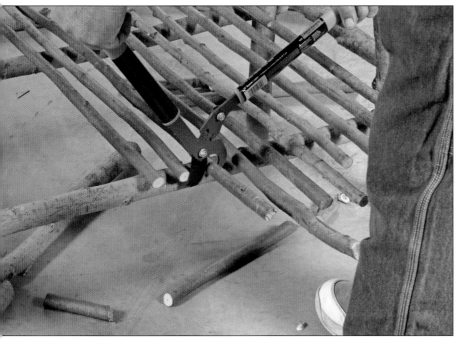

Continue adding willow until about halfway across the bottom shelf area. Then, using loppers, cut off the front ends of the overhanging willow so that they are all even at the front edge.

With pruning shears, cut off the uneven willow ends at the back of the bottom shelf.

Cut off the back ends of the overhanging willow so that they are all even at the back edge. Use these cut ends to finish building the bottom shelf.

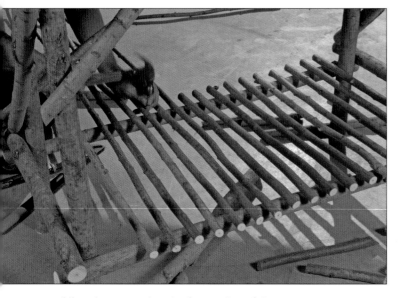

Align the cut end at the front edge of the shelf and nail into place.

To decorate the potting bench/baker's rack, I am using willow. This is when artistic expression makes the piece unique. In this case, thread the thick end of a long piece of willow inside the side brace and behind the front leg. Bend it across the side of the tabletop and top shelf, and when it is in a visually permanent location, secure it with a 6p nail at the junction of the willow with the tabletop.

Using a 4p nail, secure the thick end of the willow to the back of the front leg.

Secure it with a 6p nail.

Bend the willow top to behind the opposite back leg.

...and where it hits the back of the top shelf.

Nail the willow to the junction where it meets the top shelf...

On the other end of the table, do the same thing. Thread the thick end of a long piece of willow inside the side brace and behind the front leg. Bend it over as a mirror image of the first piece of willow trim. Nail into place wherever it hits the wood frame.

Cut off any excess.

Join pieces of the willow trim together where they cross using a 4p nail.

Lay the entire piece on the ground, with the front edge facing down. Lay out seven pieces of willow, extending below the bottom brace 6"-8" inches.

Place the middle piece of willow at the center of the bottom back brace, between the willow slats of the bottom shelf. Situate the remaining willow, three on each side, two slats apart, and spreading them into a fan pattern on the back.

Using 6p nails, secure these fan pieces in place to the bottom brace.

Using pruning shears, trim so the bottom ends are the same length, keeping the 2" Principle in mind.

Standing at the top end of the project, bend the right side piece of fanned willow toward the back right leg. Cut the fanned willow so it butts up to the inside of the top decorative loop of willow.

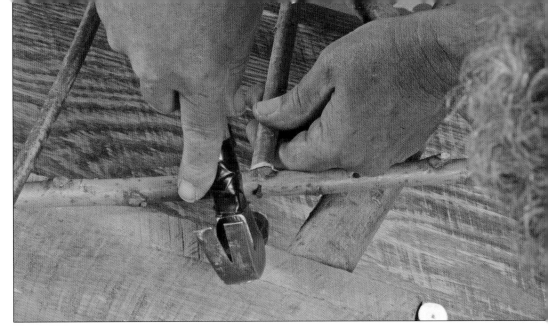

Using a 4p nail, nail
through the loop
and into the cut end
of the fan willow.

Repeat this step on the
opposite side of the project
with the left side fanned
willow and decorative loop.

Continue working
from side to side,
fanning the willow,
cutting to   fit, and
nailing in place.

For a symmetrical look, make sure that the center piece of the fanned willow is centered at the junction of the two decorative loops. The project, finished.

A close up of the bottom shelf.

The project, finished.